Those Who Are Wise

Dave Jones

TEACH Services, Inc.
P U B L I S H I N G
www.TEACHServices.com • (800) 367-1844

Copyright © 2014 Dave Jones
Copyright © 2014 TEACH Services, Inc.
ISBN-13: 978-1-4796-0310-7 (Paperback)
ISBN-13: 978-1-4796-0311-2 (ePub)
ISBN-13: 978-1-4796-0312-0 (Mobi)
Library of Congress Control Number: 2014910738

All scripture quotations, unless otherwise indicated, are taken from the New King James Version®. Copyright © 1982 by Thomas Nelson, Inc. Used by permission. All rights reserved.

The author has not attempted to dot every "i" and cross every "t" of the prophecies of Daniel. Rather, the content of this book is to provide a framework for further study of the prophetic works of Daniel and Revelation. Most important of all, it is his prayer that this work will inspire readers to walk closer with our Lord and Savior Jesus Christ in order that their name will forever remain in the Lamb's book of life!

Published by

TEACH Services, Inc.
P U B L I S H I N G
www.TEACHServices.com • (800) 367-1844

Dedication

To Dr. Julius Korgan,
whose class in ancient history
laid the foundation for this
exegesis of Daniel 11.

"And to man He said, 'Behold, the fear of the Lord, that is wisdom. And to depart from evil is understanding." Job 28:28

Table Contents

Chapter 1

By the Waters of Babylon

By the rivers of Babylon, there we sat down, yea, we wept when we remembered Zion. We hung our harps upon the willows in the midst of it. For there those who carried us away captive asked of us a song, and those who plundered us required mirth, Saying, "Sing us one of the songs of Zion!" How shall we sing the LORD's song in a foreign land? If I forget you, O Jerusalem, let my right hand forget its skill! If I do not remember you, let my tongue

cling to the roof of my mouth—if I do not exalt Jerusalem above my chief joy. Remember, O LORD, against the sons of Edom the day of Jerusalem, who said, "Raze it, raze it, to its very foundation!" O daughter of Babylon, who are to be destroyed, happy the one who repays you as you have served us!
Psalm 137:1–8

Contrary to popular opinion, Babylon was not the world's first great empire. In the antediluvian world, the earth was dominated by the influence of a city called Enoch, which was built by the world's first apostate Cain (see Gen. 4:16, 17). Eve disobeyed God when she listened to the serpent. Adam made an unwise choice when he took the fruit from Eve. But Cain disregarded God's commands, murdered his brother, refused to repent when God confronted him, and set up his own kingdom in another land.

But before banishing Cain's parents from the Garden of Eden, God gave them the promise of a coming Redeemer who would crush the serpent's head (see Gen. 3:15). Then, as if to affirm his faith in the expected Messiah, "Adam called his wife's name Eve [meaning life], because she was the mother of all living" (Gen. 3:20) and, through her lineage, would become the mother of the Savior of the world.

God placed two cherubim at the east end of the garden, with "a flaming sword which turned every way, to guard the way to the tree of life" (Gen. 3:24). Once evicted from the Garden of Eden, Adam and Eve no longer could partake of the fruit of the tree of life; however, the tree of life in heaven awaits that great day when Adam and Eve and their descendants who have been saved throughout the ages will once again be able to eat the fruit from its branches (see Rev. 22:1, 2).

No doubt Adam and Eve instructed both of their sons regarding God's plan of salvation. One can almost envision the family approaching the edges of the garden and peering inside as they rehearsed the stories concerning their fall from grace and Christ's promise of

We too should follow Abraham's example and leave the apostate philosophies and traditions of false contemporary religious concepts so that we might receive a share of his inheritance.

their redemption. By turning his back upon the only means provided for his restoration, Cain entered into a state of rebellion that clearly placed him on the side of the forces of evil, all because he wanted God to accept his form of worship instead of depending upon the Lord to become his Redeemer.

As the population of the planet increased and daughters were born, the sons of God, those who followed God in that generation, saw that the daughters of Cain's descendants were very beautiful, and they took wives for themselves. The children born to these unholy, often polygamous, relationships (see Gen. 4:19) became "the mighty men who were of old," the "men of renown" (Gen. 6:1–4).

Now we have the beginnings of a counterfeit religious system that began to mingle truth with error and resulted in the mythological deification of these so-called heroes. This became one of the primary causes of the flood.

Nimrod instituted idolatrous religious concepts after the deluge with the construction of the Tower of Babel. He was able to obtain unparalleled influence among the world's survivors because he utilized his hunting skills to help supplement their limited food supply (Gen. 10:8, 9).

Josephus, the ancient Jewish historian, relates that Shem, Ham, and Japheth were the first ones to descend from the mountains of Ararat, where the ark had settled into the plains. They encouraged others who were afraid to follow their example. But "it was Nimrod who excited them to such an affront and contempt of God. He was the grandson of Ham, the son of Noah,—a bold man, and of great strength of hand. He persuaded them not to ascribe it to God, as if it was through his means they were happy, but to believe that it was their own courage which procured that happiness. He also gradually changed the government into tyranny,—seeing no other way of turning men from the fear of God, but to bring them into a constant dependence upon his power. He also said he would be revenged on God, if he should have a mind to drown the world again; for that he would build a tower too high for the waters to be able to reach! and that he would avenge himself on God for destroying their forefathers!" (Flavius Josephus, *Antiquities of the Jews*, book 1, p. 30).

Such arrogant defiance usually receives God's special attention, and these Babel builders were no exception. In order to deal with their rebellion, the Godhead decided to confuse the world's language (Babel means confusion) and scatter humankind throughout the entire earth (Gen. 11:1–9). God had instructed them to "be fruitful and multiply, and fill the earth" (Gen. 9:1). Yet by building the city of Babel, they seemed more determined to follow Cain's example rather than to submit to the directives of the Almighty (see Isa. 5:8). Nevertheless, the construction of the tower ceased, and the Lord's desires were fulfilled by their dispersion throughout the earth.

Nimrod himself left the land of Shinar and entered the land of Assyria where he built Nineveh (Gen. 10:10, 11). From there he continued to promote and expand his religious and political aspirations.

Nimrod and his successors continued to conquer new lands and spread their influence among the people of the world. Beginning with Anatolia in the West (where the Hellenistic nations were its most ardent supporters) to Egypt in the South, and as far as India in the East, the civilized world worshipped false gods introduced by Nimrod and his descendants.

Along one of his expeditions, he met Semiramis. Although the circumstances regarding their union are somewhat conflicting, these things are certain:

- She was exceptionally smart and unusually beautiful.
- She was married to someone else when they met.
- She and Nimrod began a torrid love affair and eventually were married.

Anyone who doubts the authenticity of their relationship should consider the ancient writings of the Greek historian Diodorus Siculus and his description of the original city of Babylon. Semiramis founded the city and made it the most beautiful city on earth (Nebuchadnezzar restored it after it had been attacked by Sennacherib [see Dan. 4:30]). Babylon's walls and towers were so skillfully designed that to the eyes of the beholder they portrayed the scene of a great hunt. They were so ingeniously created that travelers approaching the city would actually think that they had wandered upon a large safari. In the midst of the fray was Semiramis riding on horseback while "hurling a javelin at a leopard," and close beside her stood "her husband Ninus," the Greek name for Nimrod, the mighty hunter, "thrusting his spear into a lion" (C. H. Oldfather, *Diodorus of Sicily*, book II, p. 379).

After erecting the walls and their gates (two of which opened up with mechanical devices), Semiramis built two palaces connected by an underground passageway. One of them was covered with animals, engraved so precisely that they actually appeared to be alive. The other palace "had bronze statues of Ninus and Semiramis and their officers, and one also of Zeus, whom the Babylonians call Belus" (Ibid., see also Jer. 50:1, 2, regarding the name of Babylon's chief god).

Semiramis also built "in the centre of the city a temple of Zeus whom, as we have said, the Babylonians call Belus" (Ibid., p. 381). The ancient historians "agree that it was exceedingly high" (Ibid.). At the top of its ascent, "Semiramis set up three statues of hammered gold, of Zeus, Hera, and Rhea" (Ibid., p. 383).

Herodotus describes its interior and ascribes it to be the temple of Jupiter Belus— Jupiter was the Roman name for Zeus (Herodotus, *The History of Herodotus,* book 1, p. 40). No doubt it was here that Nebuchadnezzar deposited the sacred articles that he had taken from the house of the one and only true God after his triumph over Jerusalem (see Dan. 1:1, 2). In so doing, he was actually declaring that Bel was superior to the Lord.

He should have recalled the words of Sennacherib's governor, Rabshakeh, when he was trying to intimidate Hezekiah by boasting about Assyria's conquests and what the angel of the Lord did as a result (see Isa. 36 and 37, especially 37:36, margin). But just as a loving Savior sent Jonah to Nineveh to save the Assyrians from destruction, our Redeemer had a plan to save the king and as many of his Babylonian subjects as possible: "Then the king instructed Ashpenaz, the master of his eunuchs, to bring some of the children of Israel and some of the king's descendants and some of the nobles, young men in whom *there was* no blemish, but good-looking, gifted in all wisdom, possessing knowledge and quick to understand, who *had* ability to serve in the king's palace, and whom they might teach the language and literature of the Chaldeans" (Dan. 1:3, 4).

Upon his death, Nimrod entrusted the keeping of what his idolatrous followers called the "Sacred Mysteries" to his wife Semiramis. She in turn induced some of the Chaldean priests from her Syrian homeland to assist her in preserving what was considered by most of the ancient world to be the true religion. The Chaldeans established a center of learning in Ur that was in existence at the time of Abraham (see Gen. 11:27–31). But the Lord called Abraham and his descendants out of Ur and led them to the Promised Land. We too should follow Abraham's example and leave the apostate philosophies and traditions of false contemporary religious concepts so that we might receive a share of his inheritance.

Like faithful Abraham, Daniel had to make a decision. The king had appointed a daily provision of his own special delicacies to eat and from the wine of his table that the young men in his service would be well cared for during their three years of training. "Now from among those of the sons of Judah were Daniel, Hananiah, Mishael, and Azariah. To them the chief of the eunuchs gave names: he gave Daniel the name Belteshazzar; to Hananiah, Shadrach; to Mishael, Meshach; and to Azariah, Abed-Nego. But Daniel purposed in his heart that he would not defile himself with the portion of the king's delicacies, nor with the wine which he drank; therefore he requested of the chief of the eunuchs that he might not defile himself. Now God had brought Daniel into the favor and goodwill of the chief of the eunuchs" (Dan. 1:6–9).

Even though the eunuch seemed to like Daniel, it was still a lot to ask of him, for he feared for his life if the king should see that the four men were paler than the other captives. Yet Daniel was able to persuade him to test them for ten days by giving them only vegetables to eat and water to drink. When the requested time was completed, these four young worthies looked better than the other students. Consequently, they were allowed to continue their special diet. And upon their graduation,

Nebuchadnezzar found them to be ten times wiser than all of the magicians, astrologers, and religious leaders (wise men) in his kingdom (see Dan. 1:5–20).

You and I, like Daniel, Hananiah, Mishael, and Azariah, are called to be witnesses for Christ to the people of spiritual Babylon. Let us exhibit the wisdom to make up our minds, just as these four worthies did, that, come what may, we will not defile ourselves with improper dress and diet, immoral and intemperate actions, or worldly culture and unholy doctrine, etc. (see Rev. 2:10). As the apostle Paul encourages us, "Therefore, whether you eat or drink, or whatever you do, do all to the glory of God" (1 Cor. 10:31). Moreover, "I beseech you therefore, brethren, by the mercies of God, that you present your bodies a living sacrifice, holy, acceptable to God, which is your reasonable service. And do not be conformed to this world, but be transformed by the renewing of your mind, that you may prove what is that good and acceptable and perfect will of God" (Rom. 12:1, 2).

The story is told of a young Christian who was arrested during the Bolshevik Revolution for her profession of the Lord Jesus Christ as her Savior from sin. When she refused to recant, the authorities threw her into prison. Yet, instead of initiating a pity party like the exiles in Psalm 137 did, she wisely determined, like Daniel and his companions, to make the best of her situation. It was not long before the guards heard her singing praises to God as Paul and Silas had done in the story recorded in Acts 16.

The warden "rewarded" her with a bucket of soap and water, exclaiming, "If you are so happy, clean up your cell!" She proceeded to sing as she cleaned, which resulted in her being released from her cell after a few days and instructed to clean up the cells of the other prisoners. Still she continued to clean and sing. After a few days, she had most of the other inmates singing with her. The result, to make a long story short, was that many of the guards and prisoners became Christians because of her example! When the governmental authorities investigated the situation, some of them also accepted the faith. Thus, that which Satan had determined to be her downfall actually became her triumphant victory!

May the Lord God enable each of us to solemnly vow to the LORD, as we confront the tests directed against us by spiritual Babylon today, that no matter what might befall us we will be faithful to Him until the end, just as this young woman and Daniel and the three Hebrews were faithful. "But he who endures to the end shall be saved" (Matt. 24:13). By the power of God, when we make the decision to stand for Him, we will not turn back.

Chapter 2

Our High Calling

And we know that all things work together for good to those who love God,
to those who are the called according
to His purpose. For whom He foreknew,
He also predestined to be conformed to
the image of His Son, that He might
be the firstborn among many brethren. Moreover whom He predestined,
these He also called; whom He called,
these He also justified, and whom
He justified, these He also glorified."
Romans 8:28–30

In the second year of his reign, King Nebuchadnezzar received a somewhat supernatural revelation. So

he summoned the religious leaders of his realm to relate this vision and explain its significance to him (see Dan. 2:1, 2). When they arrived, they besought the king in their native language to tell them what he had dreamed and they would be happy to give him its meaning. To their surprise, however, Nebuchadnezzar explained to them that he had forgotten his divine revelation, but in view of their profession to be able to communicate with the gods, he felt that relating the dream should be a very small matter to them. Furthermore, if they could ascertain the dream from the deity, he could be sure that their interpretation of it would be accurate.

Before we proceed any further with the narration of this story, let us digress for a moment in an attempt to explain the king's position based on the following points and the knowledge we have about the magicians, astrologers, sorcerers, and Chaldeans of that time:

- The magicians were religious scholars who studied, sang, and chanted sacred writings (by speaking in tongues) to supposedly ascertain the will of the gods.
- The astrologers were scientific religious leaders who studied the stars (where the gods were believed to dwell) to obtain divine direction.
- The sorcerers professed to be able to communicate with those who had died

and were thought to have passed on to the next life to be with the gods.

- The Chaldeans were the keepers of the sacred mysteries and claimed to be the spokesmen for the gods.

Thus, it was only reasonable, according to their own religious dogma, for Nebuchadnezzar to ask these religious leaders to communicate with the gods and ascertain his dream and its interpretation from them. He became completely aghast, however, when the Chaldeans were forced to admit their spiritual bankruptcy by confessing that their pretense of possessing the capability to communicate with the gods had all been a lie (see Dan. 2:10, 11).

Being of Chaldean descent himself, Nebuchadnezzar had always been taught that these priests were the mediators between the gods and humanity. Even during the glory years of the Assyrian empire, the Chaldeans had been entrusted to preserve the Babylonian religion. Now these false priests were acknowledging that they had deceived him and his people. There was only one decree for them! "For this reason the king was angry and very furious, and gave the command to destroy all the wise men of Babylon. So the decree went out, and they began killing the wise men; and they sought Daniel and his companions, to kill them" (Dan. 2:12, 13).

Daniel and his friends were considered to be religious leaders because of their training in the literature and language of the Chaldeans (Dan. 1:4). Their training appears to be in the areas of magicians and astrologers (Dan. 1:20). However, in spite of their training, we can deduce that any Hebrew willing to make an issue about diet would never have considered practicing sorcery.

King Nebuchadnezzar obviously "did not compel the Hebrew youth to renounce their faith in favor of idolatry, but he hoped to bring this about gradually" (Ellen G. White, *Prophets and Kings*, p. 481). Little did he realize that this was exactly what the one and only true God was doing with him. And now that God had exposed the spiritual impotence of the Chaldeans and their false gods, He was preparing to reveal His omnipotence to the king through Daniel. In answer to their prayers, God revealed the dream and its meaning to Daniel in a night vision.

> So Daniel blessed the God of heaven. Daniel answered and said: "Blessed be the name of God forever and ever, for wisdom and might are His. And He changes the times and the seasons; He removes kings and raises up kings; He gives wisdom to the wise and knowledge to those who have understanding. He reveals deep and secret things;

He knows what is in the darkness, and
light dwells with Him. I thank You and
praise You, O God of my fathers; You
have given me wisdom and might. and
have now made known to me what we
asked of You, for You have made known
to us the king's demand." (verses 19–23)

When Daniel returned to the king, Nebuchadnezzar inquired: "'Are you able to make known to
me the dream which I have seen, and its interpretation?'" (verse 26).

Daniel responded by giving honor to God:

"The secret which the king has demand-
ed, the wise men, the astrologers, the
magicians, and the soothsayers cannot
declare to the king. But there is a God in
heaven who reveals secrets, and He has
made known to King Nebuchadnezzar
what will be in the latter days. Your
dream, and the visions of your head
upon your bed, were these: As for you,
O king, thoughts came to your mind
while on your bed, about what would
come to pass after this; and He who reveals secrets has made known to you
what will be. But as for me, this secret
has not been revealed to me because I
have more wisdom than anyone living,

but for our sakes who make known the interpretation to the king, and that you may know the thoughts of your heart.

"You, O king, were watching; and behold, a great image! This great image, whose splendor was excellent, stood before you; and its form was awesome. This image's head was of fine gold, its chest and arms of silver, its belly and thighs of bronze, its legs of iron, its feet partly of iron and partly of clay. You watched while a stone was cut out without hands, which struck the image on its feet of iron and clay, and broke them in pieces. Then the iron, the clay, the bronze, the silver, and the gold were crushed together, and became like chaff from the summer threshing floors; the wind carried them away so that no trace of them was found. And the stone that struck the image became a great mountain and filled the whole earth. This is the dream. Now we will tell the interpretation of it before the king." (verses 27–36)

King Nebuchadnezzar knew what had transpired before the Babylonian Empire. No one had to tell him that he had led his father's armies in their conquest of Assyria. Nevertheless, like a

good leader, he was concerned about his kingdom and what would happen to it in the future.
Daniel addressed these concerns in the dream's
interpretation:

> "You, O king, are a king of kings. For
> the God of heaven has given you a
> kingdom, power, strength, and glo-
> ry; and wherever the children of men
> dwell, or the beasts of the field and
> the birds of the heaven, He has given
> them into your hand, and has made
> you ruler over them all—you are this
> head of gold. But after you shall arise
> another kingdom inferior to yours; then
> another, a third kingdom of bronze,
> which shall rule over all the earth. And
> the fourth kingdom shall be as strong
> as iron, inasmuch as iron breaks in
> pieces and shatters everything; and
> like iron that crushes, that kingdom
> will break in pieces and crush all the
> others. Whereas you saw the feet and
> toes, partly of potter's clay and partly
> of iron, the kingdom shall be divided;
> yet the strength of the iron shall be in
> it, just as you saw the iron mixed with
> ceramic clay. And as the toes of the feet
> were partly of iron and partly of clay, so
> the kingdom shall be partly strong and

partly fragile. As you saw iron mixed with ceramic clay, they will mingle with the seed of men; but they will not adhere to one another, just as iron does not mix with clay.

"And in the days of these kings the God of heaven will set up a kingdom which shall never be destroyed; and the kingdom shall not be left to other people; it shall break in pieces and consume all these kingdoms, and it shall stand forever. Inasmuch as you saw that the stone was cut out of the mountain without hands, and that it broke in pieces the iron, the bronze, the clay, the silver, and the gold—the great God has made known to the king what will come to pass after this. The dream is certain, and its interpretation is sure." (verses 37–45)

"Then King Nebuchadnezzar fell on his face, prostrate before Daniel, and commanded that they should present an offering and incense to him. The king answered Daniel, and said, 'Truly your God is the God of gods, the Lord of kings, and a revealer of secrets, since you could reveal this secret'" (Dan. 2:46, 47). Even though he had a lot to learn about the one true God, the king received a pretty thorough introduction to Him as recorded in Daniel 2. Like all other Chaldeans, Nebuchadnezzar grew up believing that the earth was eternal, without a be-ginning or an end. But now he knew that there was a God in heaven who could read men's thoughts, foretell the future, and reveal its secrets to His ser-vants the prophets. Not only were his gods false, but the kingdoms of this world were one day going to become the kingdom of God.

"Then the king promoted Daniel and gave him many great gifts; and he made him ruler over the whole province of Babylon, and chief administrator over all the wise men of Babylon. Also Daniel pe-titioned the king, and he set Shadrach, Meshach, and Abed-Nego over the affairs of the province of Babylon; but Daniel sat in the gate of the king" (Dan. 2:48, 49).

God desired that Nebuchadnezzar be brought to an understanding of the truth and have an op-portunity to follow the true God of heaven. He gives this same opportunity to all of His children.

I knew of a young man who had worked seven weeks without a day off. Although he had been brought up in the church, he had strayed away and turned his back on the God he had learned about when he was a child. As his supervisor told him that he could have the weekend off, the thought suddenly came to him, *Why don't you call your mother and tell her you're coming to church this Sabbath? It will make her very happy!*

His mother sounded as if she was going to faint when he told her the news. On Sabbath morning when his parents picked up his two daughters to take them to Sabbath School, they asked him if he was still coming with them. He assured them that he would be there as he had promised. However, when the time came for church, he reluctantly left his house. He began to doubt the wisdom of his decision to attend. Upon arriving in the church parking lot, he smoked a cigarette to get him through the service. He then reluctantly made his way to the sanctuary.

The pastor was halfway through the sermon, and to this day, the young man doesn't remember what the pastor said. However, at the end of the sermon, the pastor asked the choir to sing, and the words of the song hit the young man: "I've wandered far away from God; Lord, I'm coming home! The path of sin too long I've trod; now, I'm coming home!" Jesus spoke to that young sinner and gave him a personal invitation to become a citizen of the kingdom of God! Praise God he accepted the call!

He gives this same opportunity to all of His children.

Today, as you study this material, if you have not done so already, this same individual, now an old man, invites you to become a subject of Christ's kingdom. If Jesus could reveal himself to an idolatrous king, and a prodigal sinner, "He is able to save to the uttermost those who come to God through Him" (Heb. 7:25).

Chapter 3

A Vision of Heaven

In first year of King Belshazzar's reign, God

"'Behold, I send My messenger, and he
will prepare the way before Me. And the
Lord, whom you seek, will suddenly
come to His temple, even the Messenger
of the covenant, in whom you delight.
Behold, He is coming,' says the LORD of
hosts." Malachi 3:1

In the first year of King Belshazzar's reign, God
sent Daniel a vision. This vision confirmed the
prophecy that Daniel had already received years

before during Nebuchadnezzar's reign. But this dream also provided new insight into the future.

> Daniel spoke, saying, "I saw in my vision by night, and behold, the four winds of heaven were stirring up the Great Sea. And four great beasts came up from the sea, each different from the other. The first was like a lion, and had eagle's wings. I watched till its wings were plucked off; and it was lifted up from the earth and made to stand on two feet like a man, and a man's heart was given to it. And suddenly another beast, a second, like a bear. It was raised up on one side, and had three ribs in its mouth between its teeth. And they said thus to it: 'Arise, devour much flesh!' After this I looked, and there was another, like a leopard, which had on its back four wings of a bird. The beast also had four heads, and dominion was given to it.
>
> "After this I saw in the night visions, and behold, a fourth beast, dreadful and terrible, exceedingly strong. It had huge iron teeth; it was devouring, breaking in pieces, and trampling the residue with its feet. It was different from all the beasts that were before it,

and it had ten horns. I was considering the horns, and there was another horn, a little one, coming up among them, before whom three of the first horns were plucked out by the roots. And there, in this horn, were eyes like the eyes of a man, and a mouth speaking pompous words [great things]." (Dan. 7:1–8)

The supernatural revelation that King Nebuchadnezzar had received was in the form of an image, while this vision given to Daniel identified four great beasts. Nevertheless, the information given in both dreams was strikingly similar:

- Head of gold or lion = Babylon
- Arms/breasts of silver or bear = Medo-Persia
- Belly/thighs of brass or leopard = Greece
- Legs of iron or fourth beast = Rome

After Rome the contents of the two visions begin to differ slightly. Nebuchadnezzar's statue had feet of iron and clay, which were struck by a stone cut out without hands from the side of the mountain. This stone destroyed the great image and became a kingdom that filled the entire earth and would last forever. The dreadful/terrible fourth beast in Daniel's dream devoured its prey with huge iron teeth and stomped upon that which remained. Moreover, it had ten horns—three of which were plucked up by the roots by another little horn that spoke pompous words. Then, as Daniel was considering the horns, he was given a glimpse of heaven:

> "I watched till thrones were put in place, and the Ancient of Days was seated; His garment was white as snow, and the hair of His head was like pure wool. His throne was a fiery flame, its wheels a burning fire; a fiery stream issued and came forth from before Him. A thousand thousands ministered to Him; ten thousand times ten thousand stood before Him. The court was seated, and the books were opened." (Dan. 7:9, 10)

The apostle John further amplifies this courtroom scene in Revelation 4 and 5. After describing God (the Ancient of Days), His throne, and the twenty-four elders with their thrones, John writes about a sealed scroll with seven seals that the Father hands to Jesus to open. We believe that this scroll contains the names of the redeemed, and that Jesus, the Redeemer and Savior of the world, is the only one worthy to open the scroll, for His blood has pardoned the names in the scroll.

When a person accepts Jesus as their Savior from sin, their name is written in the book of life in heaven (Luke 10:20).

When a person accepts Jesus as their Savior from sin, their name is written in the book of life in heaven (Luke 10:20). Those who choose to reject Jesus' sacrifice and remain or return to their sinful ways will have their names blotted out of the book of life (Exod. 32:31–33; Ezek. 18). Those who are faithful until the end will receive a crown of glory, for they have chosen to be covered by the blood of the Lamb (Ezek. 18; Zech. 3; Rev. 3:5).

As Daniel contemplated the vision, he recalled the things of history that had already taken place. He remembered Babylon's conquest of Assyria and its dominance as a wealthy and fierce kingdom. He was about to witness the Medo-Persian's overthrow of Babylon. He was even aware of the emergence of Greece as the next world power. But he wanted more information about the fourth beast.

> "Then I wished to know the truth about the fourth beast, which was different from all the others, exceedingly dreadful, with its teeth of iron and its nails of bronze, which devoured, broke in pieces, and trampled the residue with its feet; and the ten horns that were on its head, and the other horn which came up, before which three fell, namely, that horn which had eyes and a mouth which spoke pompous [great] words, whose appearance was greater than

his fellows. I was watching; and the same horn was making war against the saints, and prevailing against them, until the Ancient of Days came, and a judgment was made in favor of the saints of the Most High, and the time came for the saints to possess the kingdom" (Dan. 7:19–22)

As Daniel was watching, "one like the Son of Man" came "with the clouds [angels] of heaven" before the Ancient of Days, and God gave Jesus dominion over the whole earth (verse 13, 14). Although Daniel's vision shows Jesus being given authority over the earth, it does not provide details about the judgment. That information appears in Revelation 5 where John is shown that Christ, the Lion of the tribe of Judah, comes to the Ancient of Days and receives the scroll containing the names of those who are saved. No one in heaven or on earth can open the scroll; the only one who can open it is Jesus Christ, the Lamb of God, for He conquered sin and death through His sacrifice on Calvary's cross, thus granting us our inheritance of eternal life. Think of it this way, only one equal with God could redeem us from sin, and in order for a will to be read, the testator must first die (Heb. 2:14; 9:16, 17; Rev. 5).

One of my seminary professors pointed out to us from literature contemporary to John's day that a seven-sealed book was considered then to be a last will and testament. If this is true, the courtroom scenes in Daniel 7 and Revelation 4–7 should be similar to a case in one of our probate courts, because the verdict of this pre-advent judgment results in the saints inheriting the kingdom. "For you are all sons of God through faith in Christ Jesus. For as many of you as were baptized into Christ have put on Christ. There is neither Jew nor Greek, there is neither slave nor free, there is neither male nor female; for you are all one in Christ Jesus. And if you are Christ's, then you are Abraham's seed, and heirs according to the promise" (Gal. 3:26–29).

Although we, as Christians, should look forward to the coming of Christ, our primary focus should be on the investigative judgment that is taking place now in the heavenly sanctuary as Christ prepares to receive the names of the saints who are heirs to the kingdom of God! Consider this message found in Malachi 3:

> "Behold, I sent My messenger, and he will prepare the way before Me. And the Lord, whom you seek, will suddenly come to His temple ... but who can endure the day of His coming? And who can stand when He appears? For He is like a refiner's fire and like launderers' soap. He will sit as a refiner and a

purifier of silver; He will purify the sons
of Levi, and purge them as gold and silver, that they may offer to the LORD an
offering in righteousness." (verses 1–3)

Consequently, there are two very important
points that should be of concern to every Christian:

- The seven-sealed scroll is written on the
inside and on the back. The only thing
I am aware of that was written on both
sides is the Ten Commandments, the two
tablets of the testimony (Exod. 31:18),
which means that those who have accepted the Savior will also allow Him to
cleanse them from all of their "unrighteousness" (1 John 1:9).

- The second point is more important than
the first, although it relates to it. Just as
the day came for the rains to fall and the
flood to begin, God "has appointed a day
on which He will judge the world in righteousness by the Man whom He has or-
dained" (Acts 17:31). In other words, the
time is coming in which it will be too late
for anyone to accept God's plan for our
salvation. A wise person will choose to do
so now!

Notice Zechariah's description of this salvation
process:

Then he showed me Joshua the high priest [representing God's people] standing before the Angel of the LORD [Christ], and Satan standing at his right hand to oppose him. And the LORD said to Satan, 'The LORD rebuke you, Satan! The LORD who has chosen Jerusalem rebuke you! Is this not a brand plucked from the fire?" Now Joshua was clothed with filthy garments, and was standing before the Angel.

Then He [Christ] answered and spoke to those who stood before Him, saying, "Take away the filthy garments from him." And to him He said, "See, I have removed your iniquity from you, and I will clothe you with rich robes." And I said, "Let them put a clean turban on his head." So they put a clean turban on his head, and they put the clothes on him. And the Angel of the LORD stood by.

Then the Angel of the LORD admonished Joshua, saying, "Thus says the LORD of hosts [God the Father]: 'If you will walk in My ways, and if you will keep My command, then you shall also judge My house, and likewise have charge of My courts; I will give you

places to walk among these who stand
here." (Zech. 3:1–7)

As we stand by faith before God's throne during the judgment scene in heaven, may we possess
the wisdom to accept Christ fully as our Savior,
allowing Him to remove all of our iniquity from us
and clothe us with the robes of His righteousness.
Let us be wise like Daniel and follow the guidance
of the Holy Spirit by walking in God's ways and
obeying His commands through the power of His
grace so that our names will remain in the Lamb's
book of life. If we do so, we will one day be with
Christ in heaven and walk with the heavenly beings that are witnessing this judgment scene right
now.

Chapter 4

Roman Abominations

"Then I wished to know the truth about the fourth beast, which was different from all the others, exceedingly dreadful, with its teeth of iron and its nails of bronze, which devoured, broke in pieces, and trampled the residue with its feet; and the ten horns that were on its head, and the other horn which came up, before which three fell, namely, that horn which had eyes and a mouth which spoke pompous words, whose appearance was greater than his fellows. "I was watching; and the same horn was making war against the saints, and prevailing against them, until the Ancient of Days came, and a judgment was made in favor of the saints of the Most High, and the time came for the saints to possess the kingdom." Daniel 7:19–22

Approximately two years after receiving the vision recorded in Daniel 7, the prophet was given another divine revelation, which is recorded in Daniel 8. As he was watching, he saw a ram that had two horns, one higher than the other, the highest one coming up last (Dan. 8:1–3), similar to the bear of Daniel 7:5 that was "raised up on one side." This ram symbolized the empire of the Medo-Persians, with the Persians, the strongest of this dual kingdom, emerging last (see Dan. 8:20). Daniel watched while the ram pushed westward, northward, and southward, conquering the Babylonians, the Lydians, and the Egyptians, which were represented by the three ribs in the bear's mouth. The conquest was so fierce that no one "could withstand him, nor was there any that could deliver [them] from his hand, but he did according to his will and became great" (Dan. 8:4; see also Dan. 7:5).

Persia's invasions into Grecian territory so incensed its people that they became united under

Alexander the Great and attacked them with such speed, fury, and power that the feet of the goat are described as not so much as touching the ground.

> And as I was considering, suddenly a male goat came from the west, across the surface of the whole earth, without touching the ground; and the goat had a notable horn between his eyes. Then he came to the ram that had two horns, which I had seen standing beside the river, and ran at him with furious power. And I saw him confronting the ram; he was moved with rage against him, attacked the ram, and broke his two horns. There was no power in the ram to withstand him, but he cast him down to the ground and trampled him; and there was no one that could deliver the ram from his hand. Therefore the male goat grew very great; but when he became strong, the large horn was broken, and in place of it four notable ones came up toward the four winds of heaven. (Dan. 8:5–7)

After reaching the height of his power, Alexander the Great suddenly died. Since he had no suitable heir to reign over his kingdom, it was eventually divided between his four generals: Cassander,

Seleucus, Lysimachus, and Ptolemy. Out of one of these divisions, "in the latter time of their kingdom," there "came a little horn which grew exceedingly great toward the south, toward the east, and toward the Glorious Land" (Dan. 8:9). This little horn eventually grew into the power represented by the fourth beast of Daniel 7. But before we proceed any further, let us attempt to explain why Rome is portrayed as coming up out of the Grecian empire in Daniel 8.

The founders of Babylon gave their city a name that means the gateway or the entrance way to the gods. Consequently, its priests were considered to be mediators between the gods and humankind, and they eventually began to be referred to as "bridge builders" or pontifices in Latin. They believe that it was only through the priests that the worshipper could approach the deity. The Babylonian chief priest was called the supreme or high priest (pontifex maximus in Latin). "The god" supposedly "delegated his powers to him, and allowed him to exercise them on earth" (Paul E. Quimby, *Prophetic Interpretation of Daniel and Revelation*, p. 63). Thus he became the vicegerent or spokesman for the gods.

Biblically speaking, these claims could be classified as being pompous, to say the least. There is only one mediator between God and sinful humanity, and that is Jesus Christ (1 Tim. 2:5). He alone is the faithful and true High Priest who is able to make propitiation for the sins of His people because He was tempted in all points as we are, yet without sin (Heb. 2:17, 18; 4:14–16). King Nebuchadnezzar found the Chaldeans to be guilty of speaking empty words, and any Christian who carefully conducts an honest examination of the little horn's priesthood should reach a similar conclusion. This entity has a mouth (priests) that speak great or pompous words against the Most High (Dan. 7:25).

After the Persians overthrew the Babylonian empire, the Chaldeans were forced to flee to Pergamos. The Persians considered them to be idolaters and detested some of their rituals, especially the one in which a young maiden was sent to a room in the top of their temple to spend the night with their god (Herodotus, book 1, pp. 40, 41). In His messages to the churches, Jesus Christ refers to Pergamos as being the location of Satan's seat or throne (Rev. 2:13).

The last pontiff king of Pergamos, Attalus III, willed his authority to the Romans and, beginning with Julius Caesar, this title was passed on to each succeeding emperor until Justinian delegated its power and authority to the bishop of Rome in AD 538. The pope still professes to be the Pontifex Maximus today. This apparent connection between the Roman priesthood and the Chaldeans becomes a current basis for referring to the little horn power as spiritual Babylon, which, like literal Babylon, is unable to live up to its claims.

The Persians could also be given a great deal of credit for the evolution of Sunday worship within a large portion of the Christian church. Although the Assyrians and the Babylonians worshipped their gods on religious festivals and holy days, they did not have a day set aside each week to honor their god as the servants of the Lord did. Mithraism, the Persian's mystery religion, observed Sunday as its weekly holy day in adoration of their sun god. Its followers were eventually able to persuade Emperor Constantine, shortly before his supposed conversion to Christianity, to pass legislation making Sunday a day of rest throughout the entire Roman empire (Paul E. Quimby, *Prophetic Interpretation of Daniel and Revelation*, p. 123).

The little horn's priestly hierarchy will readily admit that the seventh day is the Sabbath that God instituted at Creation, but as God's representatives here on earth, they believe they have the power to change the sanctity of the Sabbath from Saturday to Sunday. Such an attempt to change times and laws should be considered to be an additional use of pompous words in the eyes of Bible-believing Christians (see Dan. 7:25).

Perhaps the most atrocious statements ever uttered by the priests of spiritual Babylon have to do with the Eucharist. It has been defined in the dictionary as a Roman Catholic ceremony of the Last Supper in which wine and bread are consumed in remembrance of Christ's death. Listen to this doctrine as it is set forth by Cardinal Gibbons: "The sacrifice of the Mass is the consecration of the bread and wine into the body and blood of Christ, and the oblation of this body and blood to God, by the ministry of the priest, for a perpetual memorial of Christ's sacrifice on the cross. The Sacrifice of the Mass is identical with that of the cross, both having the same victim and High Priest—Jesus Christ" (*Faith of our Fathers*, p. 356, in Paul E. Quimby, *Prophetic Interpretation of Daniel and Revelation*, pp. 139, 140).

Compare Gibbon's dogma with the teachings of the apostle Paul as he explains the intercession of the true High Priest on our behalf: "And every priest stands ministering daily and offering repeatedly the same sacrifices, which can never take away sins. But this Man, after He had offered one sacrifice for sins forever, sat down at the right hand of God, from that time waiting till His enemies are made His footstool. For by one offering He has perfected forever those who are being sanctified" (Heb. 10:11–14). The Holy Spirit will make this truth evident to every sincere believer.

For 1,260 years (a time and times and half a time), from AD 538, when Justinian officially granted the bishop of Rome the title of Pontifix Maximus, until AD 1798, when Napoleon's general took the pope prisoner, the saints of God were given into the hands of spiritual Babylon (Dan. 7:21, 25). Now a message is being proclaimed by modern Daniels with a loud voice that illuminates the entire earth: "And he cried mightily with a loud voice, saying, 'Babylon the great is fallen, is fallen, and has become a dwelling place of demons, a prison for every foul spirit, and a cage for every unclean and hated bird! For all the nations have drunk of the wine of the wrath of her fornication, the kings of the earth have committed fornication with her, and the merchants of the earth have become rich through the abundance of her luxury'" (Rev. 18:2, 3).

Then John "heard another voice from heaven saying, 'Come out of her, my people, lest you share in her sins, and lest you receive of her plagues. For her sins have reached to heaven, and God has remembered her iniquities'" (Rev. 18:4, 5). Jesus said, "My sheep hear My voice, and I know them, and they follow Me" (John 10:27). As the world comes to a close, God's people, like Nebuchadnezzar when he acknowledged God as King of the universe, will heed the voice of the Savior and come out of the religious systems in which Satan has commingled truth with error since the beginning of time. For the Lord will deliver His children, everyone who is found written in the book of life (Dan. 12:1).

Chapter 5

Summer Is Nigh

"Therefore, brethren, be even more
diligent to make your call and election
sure, for if you do these things you will
never stumble; for so an entrance will
be supplied to you abundantly into the
everlasting kingdom of our Lord and
Savior Jesus Christ." 2 Peter 1:10, 11

When Daniel received the vision of chapter seven, he wanted to know the truth about the fourth beast. He did not, however, understand the heavenly being's explanation, so two years later he was given another vision. Rather than clarifying his concerns about the fourth beast, this vision recorded in chapter eight distressed the prophet so greatly that he fainted and became ill for many days. In Daniel 9 we find him in prayer and fasting, confessing his sin and the sins of his people (see verse 20).

Daniel had learned by the prophecies of Jeremiah that the desolation of Israel was only to last for seventy years (see Dan. 9:2, 2 Chron. 36:21; Jer. 25:11, 12; 29:10). What then was the meaning of the 2300 days of Daniel 8:14? The Persians were now sitting upon the Babylonian throne. Jeremiah's seventy-year prophecy was almost over. Would God forgive the children of Israel for worshipping idols and restore them to their land? In answer to his prayers Gabriel spoke with Daniel and told him the meaning of the vision: "Seventy weeks are determined for your people and for your holy city, to finish the transgression, to make an end of sins, to make reconciliation for iniquity, to bring in everlasting righteousness, to seal up vision and prophecy, and to anoint the Most Holy" (Dan. 9:24).

Just as the LORD had called Abraham out of Ur, out of the center of the idolatrous worship of the Chaldean religion, He was preparing to restore His children and rebuild Jerusalem. This wasn't the first time that God had rescued His people from a land of false gods and false worship. He sent Moses to lead the children of Israel out of Egypt; however, the people reverted back to their idolatrous ways by building a golden calf despite the manifestation of God's power at Sinai following their deliverance from bondage. Then He sustained them in the wilderness for nearly forty years with food, water, and shelter only to watch them "commit harlotry with the women of Moab.... So Israel was joined to Baal of Peor" (Num. 25:1, 3). The biblical narrative of the children of Israel in the Promised Land is one of revival followed by apostasy.

From the time they crossed over the Jordan and conquered the Canaanite citadel of idolatry at Jericho, there were those who, like Achan, coveted the garments of the Babylonian religion.

History repeats itself, for we find similar conditions throughout the history of the Christian church. It sometimes appears as though the majority of humankind, even among the professed people of God, would rather believe a lie instead of the truth. This just seems to be a part of our sinful natures. Yet each of us has a choice; a choice to heed the warnings of God's prophets and reformers or disregard the divine instruction.

The angel Gabriel continued: "Know therefore and understand, that from the going forth of the command to restore and build Jerusalem until Messiah the Prince, there shall be seven weeks and sixty-two weeks; the street shall be built again, and the wall, even in troublesome times" (Dan. 9:25). In 457 BC the Persians issued a decree allowing the children of Israel to restore and rebuild Jerusalem (see Ezra 7). Forty-nine years (seven prophetic weeks) later, Jerusalem and the temple were rebuilt.

Four hundred eighty-three years (seven plus sixty-two weeks) after this decree went forth, Jesus was baptized and began preaching: "The time is fulfilled, and the kingdom of God is at hand. Repent, and believe the gospel!" (Mark 1:15). Sadly, instead of repenting of their sins and making things right with God by accepting Jesus as the Messiah, they crucified the Lamb of God. He came unto His own chosen people in fulfillment of Daniel's prophecy, and they refused to receive Him (see John 1:11).

However, before we condemn the Jews for their rejection of the Savior, we should reconsider the apostasy and errors that have crept into the Christian church. Praise be to God that He is saving individuals instead of nations, institutions, and/ or religious systems! "Whoever calls on the name of the LORD shall be saved" (Acts 2:21).

The chronology of Gabriel's interpretation of the visions Christ gave to the prophet Daniel are as follows:

1. The seventy weeks (490 years) were a distinct unit of time given to the children of Israel to get right with God.

2. The prophecy began in 457 BC and culminated in AD 34 when the Holy Spirit selected a remnant of the Jewish people to carry the gospel to the Gentile nations and formulate the Christian church.

3. In the middle of the seventieth week, Christ was crucified ("cut off") to pay for the sins of the entire world. Thus, by so doing, He put an end to the sacrificial system that pointed forward to His death for our sins (see Daniel 9:26, 27).

4. Furthermore, as we have previously pointed out, the visions begin with Babylon (who conquered Assyria), through Persia, then Greece, followed by Rome, to the judgment, culminating with the coming of Christ and the establishment of the kingdom of God.

Thus, the 490 years is obviously a part of the 2300-year prophecy. Both time prophecies began in 457 BC. The 490 years of Jewish probation ended in AD 34, and the 2300 years ended in 1844 when the judgment officially began in the heavenly sanctuary. Even after AD 34, the Lᴏʀᴅ, in tender mercy, compassionately extended the time granted to the Jewish nation before allowing the Romans to destroy their temple in AD 70 and their holy city of Jerusalem in AD 135.

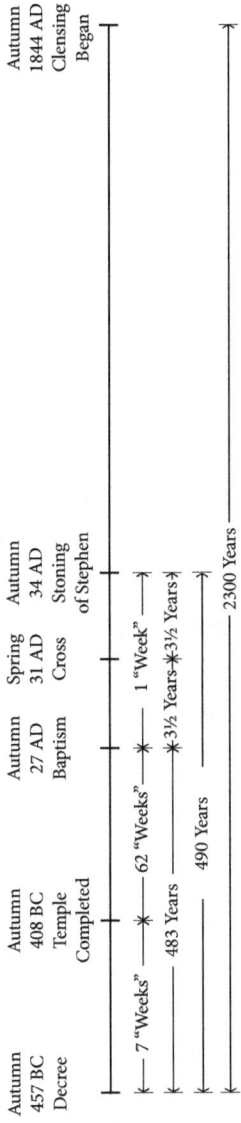

Autumn 457 BC — Decree
Autumn 408 BC — Temple Completed
Autumn 27 AD — Baptism
Spring 31 AD — Cross
Autumn 34 AD — Stoning of Stephen
Autumn 1844 AD — Clensing Began

7 "Weeks"
62 "Weeks"
1 "Week"
3½ Years — 3½ Years
483 Years
490 Years
2300 Years

Similarly, our time of probation has been gracefully prolonged since 1844. Yet God "has appointed a day on which He will judge the world in righteousness" according to their allegiance to our Lord and Savior Jesus Christ or the prince of darkness (Acts 17:31; see also Rev. 13:11–14:16). Those who die before the close of probation will be saved based on their reception of the light they have received (see Rom. 1:18–20).

As it was in the days of Noah, so also will be the close of probation and the coming of Christ: "For as in the days before the flood, they were eating and drinking, marrying and giving in marriage, until the day that Noah entered the ark, and did not know until the flood came and took them all away, so also will the coming of the Son of Man be" (Matt. 24:37–39). For 120 years Noah preached of an impending judgment. Yet since it had never rained, very few people believed him, for they could not envision a flood. Along with the animals, Noah and seven other members of his family entered the ark, but no one else joined him. Then an unseen hand shut the door. Still, nothing happened for seven days, but then the rains came and the flood destroyed the entire earth and all the people and animals who were not in the ark.

The judgment is now taking place in heaven. God has warned us in the Bible of the impending destruction of the earth. Will we heed the warnings God has given us or wait until it is too late? "Then the kingdom of heaven shall be likened to ten virgins who took their lamps [Bibles] and went out to meet [Christ] the bridegroom. Now five of these virgins were wise, and five were foolish" (Matt. 25:1, 2). The wise carried their lamps along with extra oil, representing the Holy Spirit. The foolish also had their lamps, but they carried no extra oil with them. The bridegroom delayed His coming, and all ten of the virgins fell asleep.

"And at midnight [just before the end of the world] a cry was heard: 'Behold, the bridegroom [Jesus] is coming; go out to meet him!' Then all those virgins arose and trimmed their lamps" (verses 6 and 7). But the foolish ones discovered that they were running short of oil. They asked the wise virgins to sell them some of their extra oil, but the wise ones had just enough for themselves. Therefore, they encouraged the foolish ones to purchase what they needed, which they tried to do, except they did not have enough time left to do so. The wise virgins who were ready went into the marriage, and "the door was shut" (verse 10).

Jesus also told the parable of the fig tree as a reminder to those who hear it to be ready for His coming: "Now learn this parable from the fig tree: When its branch has already become tender and puts forth leaves, you know that summer is near" (Matt. 24:32).

The world before the flood should have learned that summer was near through Noah's preaching and the miraculous sign of the animals marching into the ark. The prophet Daniel was given definite dates and signs that the Israelites should have heeded and acknowledged that Jesus was indeed the Messiah, as many wise Jews recognized after His resurrection. And although the judgment is taking place now in heaven, Scripture reveals that it began in 1844, and there are ample signs to inform us that its conclusion is rapidly approaching.

In the next chapter we will discuss some of these signs Daniel recorded for the Jewish nation regarding the 490 years of their probation. And we will conclude this work with some signs that pertain to the Christian church and the conclusion of the investigative judgment so that we are prepared like the wise virgins.

Chapter 6

Understanding the Vision

"Although I heard, I did not understand. Then I said, 'My lord, what shall be the end of these things?' And he said, 'Go your way, Daniel, for the words are closed up and sealed till the time of the end. Many shall be purified, made white, and refined, but the wicked shall do wickedly; and none of the wicked shall understand, but the wise shall understand." Daniel 12:8–10

In order for us to gain a better understanding of Daniel 11, it is important to keep in mind the following details as we begin this chapter and move into the next chapter of this book.

- Daniel's vision of chapter 7 expands and amplifies Nebuchadnezzar's dream in chapter 2.
- The vision Daniel received in chapter 8 clarifies some of his concerns in chapter 7 regarding the fourth beast (see Dan. 7:19, 20; 8:1).
- The events recorded in the vision of Daniel 11 were given to enable him to comprehend what would happen to his people in the last days (see Dan. 10:14).

As we continue this study, it is important to remember the accumulated events and sequence of the kingdoms that appear in the book of Daniel:

- Assyria – previously conquered by Babylon.
- Babylon – passing off the scene in Daniel 8 and already irrelevant in chapter 11.
- Persia – only lists four remaining kings because it was just a matter of time before Greece would defeat Darius III and Persia after what Darius I and Xerxes (Ahasuerus) had done by invading them.
- Greece – mentioned in Daniel 11:3–15.
- Rome – mentioned in Daniel 11:16–28.

- Spiritual Babylon – this is the little horn of chapters 7 and 8; see also Daniel 11:29–39.
- Judgment – mentioned in Daniel 7:9–14 and 11:40–45.
- Deliverance – mentioned in Daniel 12:1.
- God's Kingdom – mentioned in Daniel 7:26, 27.

One must also keep in mind that the 490 years of Israel's probation began under Persia in 457 BC and ended under the rule of the Roman Empire. God used them to inflict judgment upon His people by destroying their temple in AD 70 and

Everyone whose name remains written in the book of life will be saved at His appearing.

their holy city in AD 135. After which He dispersed the Jews throughout the world in fulfillment of Deuteronomy 31:14–22 and 32:1–43.

Since 1844 the Lord has been gathering all of His people (both Jews and Gentiles) together from their exile in spiritual Babylon and preparing them for their deliverance. Everyone whose name remains written in the book of life will be saved at His appearing.

Daniel received his initial vision in the first year of Belshazzar's reign. It was amplified and explained again to him during the third year of this king's administration. The prophet then received further prophetic details in the first year of the

King Darius' rule. Now we observe him obtaining an additional understanding in the third year of the reign of King Cyrus (see Dan. 10:1).

In this vision Gabriel begins his interpretation by informing the prophet that "three more kings will arise in Persia, and the fourth shall be far richer than them all; by his strength, through his riches, he shall stir up all against the realm of Greece" (Dan. 11:2). The three rulers who followed Cyrus were Cambyses, Gaumata, and Darius I. The fourth monarch, Ahasuerus (Xerxes) of the book of Esther, mustered a vast army from more than forty different nations in order to invade the Greek peninsula. He did not succeed in his conquest; instead, he infuriated the Greeks so much that they quickly united in an effort to crush the Persian Empire.

Alexander the Great led his armies against the Persian forces with such fury that with leopard-like speed it appeared that they did not touch the ground (see Dan. 7:6; 8:5–7). Nevertheless, when Alexander the Great died suddenly at the age of 32, he left his kingdom under the control of his four generals. The king of the South, Ptolemy, became strong, along with Seleucus, the king of the North (see Dan. 11:5). After a long and costly war between the two kings, in an effort to reunite the empire, Ptolemy II gave his daughter, Berenice, in marriage to Antiochus II. In order to do this, Antiochus divorced his wife Laodice. Instead of accomplishing the reunification of the Greek Empire, however, Berenice and many of her attendants from Egypt were mysteriously murdered, most likely by Laodice (Dan. 11:6).

So once again there was conflict between the kings of the North and the South. Ptolemy III, Berenice's brother, invaded the Seleucid Empire, defeated Seleucus II and pushed him back into Asia Minor. Yet, instead of taking advantage of this victory by controlling the territory and reuniting the Greek Empire, he returned to Egypt with the spoils of war (Dan. 11:7, 8).

Seleucus II eventually regrouped and invaded Egypt again, only to be defeated by Ptolemy III a second time. After his death and the murder of his son Seleucus III, his other son, Antiochus the Great (Antiochus III) mustered an army of 62,000 soldiers, 6,000 cavalry, and 102 elephants in an attempt to defeat Egypt once and for all (see *The SDA Bible Commentary,* vol. 4, p. 868).

Angered by the audacity of the Seleucids at-tempting to conquer Egypt once again after the defeats they suffered at the hands of his father, Ptolemy IV attacked Antiochus III at Rephia, along the Egyptian/Palestine border, in 217 BC. He had a similar size army, and he soundly defeated him, killing 10,000 infantry, 300 cavalry, and taking 4,000 prisoners (Ibid.).

Antiochus III returned, however, when the child king Ptolemy V ascended to the Egyptian throne (204 BC) with an even greater army in 201 BC. It appeared as if Egypt was about to experience certain doom as Antiochus III began to conquer Egyptian controlled territory in Palestine. Yet, the closer he got to Egypt, the more he became intimidated by Rome, and in 190 BC the Romans defeated him and took the Seleucid territory west of the Taurus Mountains (Ibid., p. 823). His massive invasion, therefore, only resulted in a few minor victories. Egypt was powerless to attack him; nevertheless, he, for whatever reason, failed to attack Egypt (Dan. 11:9–13).

No more is said in Scripture about any additional conflicts between the kings of the North and the South after Daniel 11:15. The events of verse 14, however, do appear to refer to Antiochus Epiphanes taking out his frustrations against Rome upon Israel. (One can read about these exploits in the Books of the Maccabees.) They were only magnified when a Roman ambassador delievered the message that if he invaded Egypt he would be at war with Rome. Still, the Romans (under Pompey) completely defeated the Seleucids in 63 BC.

Somewhere along the line, Rome begins to become the protagonist. Not every detail is listed, neither is each item foretold in the vision, but we do know the following: "But he who comes against him [the king of the North] shall do according to his own will, and no one shall stand against him. He shall stand in the Glorious Land with destruction in his power. He shall also set his face to enter with the strength of his whole kingdom, and up-right ones with him; thus shall he do" (Dan. 11:16, 17).

Then Cleopatra ascended the throne of Egypt as the last pharaoh. She began her reign in 51 BC. In a political move to solidify her power, she became romantically involved with Julius Caesar. Upon his assassination in 44 BC, Cleopatra turned her attentions to Mark Antony, one of Caesar's generals. Caesar's heir, Gaius Julius Caesar Octavianus, responded to their union by assembling his army to attack Cleopatra and Mark Antony's forces. The Battle of Actium ensued, and Octavian defeated them, thus securing his reign of Rome as the only son of Caesar. Following Mark Antony and Cleopatra's suicides, Egypt became part of the Roman Empire and the Ptolemaic Kingdom was dissolved (Dan. 11:17-19 & 25–28).

After becoming emperor, Caesar Augustus imposed a tax upon the entire world, including Israel, demonstrating that they were no longer his allies but his subjects (see Luke 2:1–3). One would think that this would have been a wake up call to the Israeli nation that the 490-year prophecy of Daniel was almost ending and the Messiah was soon to come. However, their day of judgment crept upon them unawares, and the Romans not only crucified the Messiah, but they destroyed the Jewish nation. "After the league [agreement] is made with him [Rome] he shall act deceitfully, for he shall come up and become strong with a small number of people. He shall enter peacefully, even into the richest places of the province; and he shall do what his fathers have not done, nor his forefathers; he shall disperse among them the plunder, spoil, and riches; and he shall devise his plans against the strongholds, but only for a time" (Dan. 11:23, 24; see also verses 17–28).

Beginning in 31 BC, when the Roman Empire was established, until AD 330, a total of 360 years, when Emperor Constantine moved the capital from Rome to Constantinople, a variety of events took place.

- The nation of Israel became subservient to the Roman Empire
- The Romans crucified the Messiah
- Rome destroyed the Jewish temple in AD 70
- Jerusalem was destroyed in AD 135 and rebuilt by Emperor Hadrian as a Roman city
- The children of Israel were dispersed throughout the earth

Under the direction of the Roman emperors, from Nero to Diocletian, both Jews and Christians were persecuted. At this time Christianity was considered to be a part of Judaism because it had been founded by Jews. In order to avoid persecution, many Christians renounced their Jewish roots. This led to countless errors creeping into the church. Further errors became accepted as truth when Emperor Constantine was converted to Christianity (see Dan. 11:29–39), and church and state were unified and the Roman Catholic Church was formed.

"At the appointed time he [Rome] shall return and go toward the south; but it shall not be like the former or the latter. For ships from Cyprus shall come against him; therefore he shall be grieved, and return in rage against the holy covenant [the Ten Commandments, see Deut. 4:13], and do damage So he shall return and show regard for those who forsake the holy covenant" (Dan. 11:29, 30).

The term "ships from Cyprus" seems to be the way God chose to reveal to Daniel who the ten Germanic tribes that invaded the Roman Empire were. They are considered to be the Ostrogoths, Visigoths, Franks, Vandals, Suevi, Alemanni, Anglo-Saxons, Heruli, Lombards, and Burgundians. Daniel was now living under the reign of Persia. He probably had some knowledge of Greece. He might even have had a limited conception of Rome. But it is doubtful that these ten tribes even existed while Daniel was alive. Hence, the use of this term to refer to the fact that they came into the Roman Empire from the west.

Three of these tribes—the Heruli, Vandals, and Ostrogoths—were "plucked out" by the united efforts of the bishop of Rome and the emperor because they were a direct threat to the city of Rome.

The remaining seven along with the little horn continued to rule the western sections of the Roman Empire. It is important to note, therefore, that the fourth beast is still under the control of these eight remaining horns today.

During the Middle Ages, from AD 538–1798, the civil powers united in various ways with spiritual Babylon to support her pompous words (see Dan. 7:20, 25), to defile the heavenly sanctuary by casting down its truths to the ground (see Dan. 8:11, 12), and to attempt to claim equality with God (see Dan. 8:23–26; 11:32–39).

Nevertheless, God is still seated upon His throne in His holy temple! "The Lord is in His holy temple, the Lord's throne is in heaven; His eyes behold, His eyelids test the sons of men" (Ps. 11:4). False religious systems view things through human eyes, but God's eyes behold and test everything. God has a surveillance device that defies human imagination. It not only records our actions, but it also is capable of recording our thoughts and emotions.

"The Lord tests the righteous, but the wicked and the one who loves violence His soul hates. Upon the wicked He will rain coals; fire and brimstone and a burning wind shall be the portion of their cup. For the Lord is righteous, He loves righteousness; His countenance beholds the upright" (Ps. 11:5–7).

Those who choose to follow God and His Word will receive the gift of eternal life.

Chapter 7

Delivering Us From Sin

"Those who are wise shall shine like the brightness of the firmament, and those who turn many to righteousness like the stars forever and ever." Daniel 12:3

Thousands of years ago a "war broke out in heaven: Michael [Christ] and his angels fought with the dragon; and the dragon and his angels fought, but they did not prevail, nor was a place found for them in heaven any longer. So the great dragon was cast out, that serpent of old, called the Devil and Satan, who deceives the whole world; he was cast to the earth, and his angels were cast out with him" (Rev. 12:7–9).

The first battle between Satan and human beings took place in the Garden of Eden. Disguising himself as a serpent, which was the most intelligent beast of God's creation, the devil enticed Eve into eating fruit from the forbidden tree of the knowledge of good and evil. This skirmish continued when Eve became Satan's agent and convinced her husband to partake of its fruit also, an act that resulted in bringing sin and death into the world (see Gen. 3:1–19; Rom. 5:12–19).

The next major conflict that involved the devil's temptations resulted when their eldest son, Cain, killed his brother, Abel, following a religious dispute between the two young men regarding the correct system of worship. Instead of repenting for his sins, Cain chose to leave the land of his father and the presence of the LORD and set up his own city in the land of Nod, which was east of Eden (Gen. 4:16)

For a time the righteous descendants of Adam attempted to persuade the rebellious followers of Cain to repent and accept Christ's provision for their salvation. However, Satan eventually seduced many of the "sons of God" to enter into polygamous relationships with the worldly "daughters of men," Cain's descendants (Gen. 6:2). As a result of the wickedness of humanity, the LORD sent a flood to destroy the world and its inhabitants (see

Gen. 3:25–9:17). Of course, God provided a way of escape. He sent Noah to preach to the people and offer them salvation by entering the ark. Sadly, only Noah and his family believed God and prepared for the flood.

After the deluge, as the human race began to once again multiply upon the face of the earth, the devil used the defiant Nimrod to entice people to build another city, this time with a tower that would reach to the heavens so that they could escape if another flood came. God confounded the language of the people, and the construction of the Tower of Babel was brought to a stop (Gen. 11:1–9). Furthermore, this forced humanity to scatter across the face of the earth. Realizing that his plans to develop a one-world government had been foiled, Nimrod went into the land of Assyria and built the city of Nineveh.

As the population of the earth continued to increase, the Assyrian Empire became stronger and stronger. However, God still had His true followers among the unrighteous. He called Abraham out of the land of Ur of the Chaldeans, only to have Satan enslave Abraham's descendants in Assyria's vassal state of Egypt. God responded by commissioning Moses to deliver the children of Israel from their Egyptian bondage and escorting them into the Promised Land. Yet, instead of allowing Him to make them a great nation by faithfully following His covenant, the Israelites vacillated between serving the one true God and false idolatrous gods. As a result of Israel's apostasy, Assyria and other people groups of Canaan threatened and attacked the nation at times.

When the Babylonians eventually destroyed the temple and the Jewish nation, the devil must have felt victorious. However, his joy was short lived, for God had a loyal follower in Daniel and his three friends. Through their faithfulness, they converted many of Babylon's citizens, including the king, to worship the one true God.

After Persia set the Israeli captives free, Satan inspired Haman the Agagite to obtain permission from the king to pass a new decree allowing him to execute all of the Jews. However, God thwarted these plans as well. This time He used a maiden, Esther, to save His people.

Moving forward in time, we see the destruction of Persia by Alexander the Great and his Greek army. After Alexander's death, God's people were not quite as fortunate. The incessant warfare that existed between the Ptolemies and the Selucids after the division of the Greek Empire wreaked havoc in the land of Israel. Of course, the Roman Empire, which came on the heels of the Greeks, also oppressed the Jews.

However, the Lord had plans for His people. God sent His Son into the world to save humanity from sin. Even though Satan successfully led the Jewish leaders to kill Him, the Father resurrected Him and used His disciples to establish the Christian church. The Roman persecution that followed resulted in the rapid growth of Christianity. Consequently, the devil was forced to come up with another plan. He had accomplished his goals by leading God's people into apostasy in the past, why not bring similar errors into the Christian church?

For 1260 years ("a time and times and half a time), from the time that Emperor Justinian gave the bishops of Rome the title of chief pontiff in AD 538 until General Berthier stripped the Vatican of the papal states and took the pope prisoner in 1798, Satan used so-called Christians to war against God's true believers (see Dan. 7:25). Many Christians paid for their fidelity to God with their lives, which brings us down to the final conflict shaping up to take place in our day: "At the time of the end [considered to be 1798] the king of the South shall attack [push at, KJV] him [the fourth beast under the control of the eight remaining horns]; and the king of the North shall come against him [the western powers] like a whirlwind, with chariots, horsemen, and with many ships; and he [the western powers] shall enter the countries, overwhelm *them,* and pass through" (Dan. 11:40).

"A French invasion in 1798 lasted only a few years but brought Egypt into the world of European politics. After the departure of the French, the government passed into the hands of Muhammad 'Ale, probably an Albanian, who created a dynasty and an empire nominally under Ottoman control" (*Encyclopedia Britannica*, vol. 4, p. 390). The Ottoman Empire (the king of the North) was created by Turkish tribes in Anatolia that lasted from the decline of the Byzantine Empire in the fourteenth century until the establishment of Turkey as a republic in 1922 (Ibid., vol. 9, p. 6). Through war, alliances, and territorial purchases, they expanded their empire from Iran on the east, through the Middle East and the remnants of the Seleucid Empire, and as far west as the Danube in Europe. "The Balkan wars of 1912–13 all but completed the empire's expulsion from Europe" (Ibid.). They suffered a disastrous defeat in World War I, after which the western powers (primarily the English) entered into much of their land.

Daniel 11:41–44 gives us the following insight: "He [the eight-horned power] shall also enter the Glorious Land, and many countries shall be overthrown; but these shall escape from his hand: Edom, Moab, and the prominent people of Ammon [Jordan]. He shall stretch out his hand against the countries, and the land of Egypt shall not escape. He shall have power over the treasures of gold and silver, and over all the precious things of Egypt [many of their valuable artifacts were taken to the museums of the Western nations]; also the Libyans and Ethiopians [Africans who were enslaved] shall follow at his heels. But news from the east and the north shall trouble him; therefore he shall go out with great fury to destroy and annihilate many."

Let's consider verse 44, which states the "news from the east and the north shall trouble him." Directly east of Palestine lies Jordan. East of Jordan is Iraq, which is experiencing much unrest. East of Iraq is Iran, a country that many Western nations are concerned about because of nuclear weapons. On the east of Iran is Afghanistan, a country at war. North of Palestine is Syria, another country in turmoil. Without a doubt the Middle East is a cause of concern in the Western world. But if the problems presented by these rogue nations do not arouse enough alarm within us, try going straight northeast from Palestine until you reach the border between eastern Syria and western Iraq: the sparsely populated area presently being occupied by Islamic State of Iraq and Syria (ISIS). Is verse 44 being fulfilled right before our very eyes?

If we look at verse 45, we find another definite sign: "And he shall plant the tents of his palace between the seas and the glorious holy mountain; yet he shall come to his end, and no one will help him." The extension of a nation's palace (seat of government) is its embassy. All of the Western nations have their embassies located in Jerusalem, including the Vatican, except for the United States. Its embassy is located in Tel Aviv. All attempts to move it, including the passing of the Jerusalem

Embassy Act of 1995 by the 104th Congress, have failed. Could this be part of God's act of holding back the winds of strife until the sealing of His servants (see Rev. 7:1–3)?

The sign, seal, or mark of God is His holy Sabbath day (see Ezek. 20:12, 20). John prophesies that this mark will become one of the final tests of God's people before the end of the world (see. Rev. 13:11–17; 14:9–12). Those who remain faithful to God and His holy Sabbath day will be saved. Those who choose to place human traditions above the Word of God will be lost (see Rev. 14:14–20).

While extreme caution should be used when attempting to interpret unfulfilled prophecy, after Daniel 11:45 is fulfilled, Christ will stand up and "And there shall be a time of trouble, such as never was since there was a nation, even to that time. And at that time your people shall be delivered, every one who

> *And at that time your people shall be delivered, every one who is found written in the book"* (Dan. 12:1).

is found written in the book" (Dan. 12:1). It is important, therefore, for us to be aware that our redemption is drawing near. Although this may seem frightening, it is consoling to note that the Lord will deliver everyone whose name is written in the book of life! Thus, our prayer should ever be, "Thank you, Jesus, for this precious promise! Blot out my sins (see Acts 3:19). Cleanse me from all unrighteousness (see 1 John 1:9). And confess my name before Your Father and His holy angels (see Rev. 3:5), so that my name will forever remain in Your book of life."

We invite you to view the complete
selection of titles we publish at:

www.TEACHServices.com

Scan with your mobile
device to go directly
to our website.

Please write or email us your praises, reactions, or
thoughts about this or any other book we publish at:

TEACH Services, Inc.
P U B L I S H I N G
www.TEACHServices.com ● (800) 367-1844

P.O. Box 954
Ringgold, GA 30736

info@TEACHServices.com

TEACH Services, Inc., titles may be purchased in bulk for
educational, business, fund-raising, or sales promotional use.
For information, please e-mail:

BulkSales@TEACHServices.com

Finally, if you are interested in seeing
your own book in print, please contact us at

publishing@TEACHServices.com

We would be happy to review your manuscript for free.